Table of Contents

Introduction

Try some French Canadian Breakfasts…

   1 – Canadian Crepes

   2 – Quebec Cretons & Toast

   3 – Maple Syrup Grandfathers

Tempting Quebec Dinner and Side Dish recipes…

   4 – French Canadian Meat Tourtière

   5 – Quebec-Style Poutine

   6 – Montreal Caramelized Apples

   7 – Quebec Meatball & Pork Shank Stew

   8 – French Canadian Gougeres

   9 – Quebec-Style Maple Baked Beans

   10 – French Canadian Bagels

   11 – Quebec Split Pea Soup

   12 – French Canadian Cauliflower Soup

   13 – Slow Cooker-Style Ham with Maple Syrup & Beer

   14 – Montreal-Style Cranberry Relish

   15 – Savory Chicken Pies

   16 – French Canadian Onion Soup

   17 – Shepherd's Pie

   18 – Montreal Pork Pie

   19 – Quebec Pork Roast

20 – Montreal Squash Bisque

21 – Quebec Maple Smash Drink

22 – Canadian Brie & Syrup

23 – Quebec Garlic Soup

24 – French Canadian Cheese Fondue

25 – French Onion Pie

Check out these Delectable Desserts from Quebec…

26 – French Canadian Cinnamon Pastry

27 – Apple Cider Quebec Pound Cake

28 – French Canadian Maple Syrup Pie

29 – Quebec Sugar Pie

30 – French Canadian Poor Man's Pudding

Conclusion

Thank You!

Introduction

What's the best way for you to create tasty Quebec dishes with ingredients that are the same or quite similar to those used in recipes in the Canadian province?

Just thumb through the amazing recipes in this illustrated cookbook.

How do French Canadian ingredients lend themselves to delicious meals in other parts of the world?

Quebec has had its own identity, cuisine-wise, for a longer period of time than most provinces in Canada. The agriculture industry is protected by the province, so chefs and home cooks alike there have easy access to a myriad of local ingredients that allow them to prepare tasty and original Québécois dishes.

Quebec was among the first-settled Canadian provinces. Much of their cuisine was influenced by the culinary traditions of French settlers, using ingredients found locally in Quebec. The recipes brought from France evolved to include local seafood, meats and agricultural products.

Cheese is used extensively in French Canadian cooking and has become an important part of the local economy.

Read on to learn more and try your hand at authentic Quebec recipes!

Try some French Canadian Breakfasts...

1 – Canadian Crepes

The crepes made in French Canadian provinces are wonderful and delicate for breakfast. Their edges are crispy, and they taste best with fruit sauce or maple syrup.

Makes 6 Servings

Cooking + Prep Time: 35 minutes

Ingredients:

- 2 cups of flour, all-purpose
- 1/4 tsp. of salt, kosher
- 2 cups of milk, whole
- 2 eggs, large
- Shortening, as needed
- To serve: maple syrup

Instructions:

In large bowl, combine the flour with kosher salt. Whisk in the milk and eggs till you have formed a thin batter.

Place 2 tbsp. shortening in large, cast-iron skillet on med. heat. After shortening heats, pour some batter from step 1 in center of pan. Swirl it around so it forms a large-sized crepe.

Cook each crepe for 1 to 2 minutes each side. Continue till you have used all the batter and serve along with syrup.

2 – Quebec Cretons & Toast

Cretons is a type of meat spread, usually made with pork, that is especially popular in French Canadian provinces. It is typically served on multi-grain bread or toast.

Makes 12 Servings

Cooking + Prep Time: 1 & 1/2 hours

Ingredients:

- 1 lb. of pork, ground
- 1 cup of milk, 2%
- 1 chopped onion, medium
- Chopped garlic, as desired
- Salt, kosher & pepper, ground, as desired
- A pinch of allspice, ground
- A pinch of cloves, ground
- 1/4 cup of breadcrumbs, dry

Instructions:

Place pork, onions, garlic and milk in large pan. Season using kosher salt, ground pepper, allspice and cloves.

Cook mixture on med. heat for 55-60 minutes. Stir in breadcrumbs. Cook for 8-10 minutes more. Adjust the seasonings as desired. Serve on toast.

3 – Maple Syrup Grandfathers

Also called Grands-Peres a L'erable, these hot sweet dumplings are eaten with maple syrup and occasionally with ice cream. They are usually eaten at breakfast-time or as a dessert.

Makes 4 Servings

Cooking + Prep Time: 1 hour & 5 minutes

Ingredients:

To Make the Dumplings:

- 2 to 2 & 1/4 cups of flour, all-purpose
- 1 tbsp. of baking powder, pure
- 1/2 tsp. of cinnamon, ground
- A pinch of salt, kosher
- 3 tbsp. of butter, unsalted
- 3/4 cup of milk, whole

To Make the Cooking Liquid:

- 1 & 1/2 cups of water, filtered
- 2 cups of syrup, maple

Instructions:

In large mixing bowl, combine flour, starting with 2 cups, with baking powder. Stir well. Add 1 tbsp. of cinnamon and 1 pinch salt. Whisk together well.

Add the butter. Cut into flour using pastry cutter till butter has become pea sized. Add milk. Mix together, adding more flour if needed, till you have the consistency of a wet dough for bread-making.

Add filtered water to wide pot. Add maple syrup and bring mixture to simmer.

Drop in dough balls one after another. Gently simmer for 15-20 minutes or so. Serve plain, with ice cream or in cooking liquid

Tempting Quebec Dinner and Side Dish recipes…

4 – French Canadian Meat Tourtière

This is one of the most commonly prepared Quebec comfort food dishes. It is enjoyed frequently during the holiday season.

Makes 8 Servings

Cooking + Prep Time: 2 hours & 20 minutes + 1 hour chilling time

Ingredients:

- 1 pie crust, prepared
- Canadian steak seasoning, prepared

For the Filling:

- 1 peeled & quartered large potato, Russet
- 2 tsp. + a couple pinches of salt, kosher
- 1 tbsp. of butter, unsalted, frozen slices
- Vinegar, cider, as needed
- 1 finely chopped onion, large
- 4 crushed garlic cloves

- 1/2 cup of celery, diced finely
- 1 lb. of beef, ground
- 1 lb. of veal, ground
- 1 cup of reserved cooking water from potatoes, + extra if needed

For the Egg Wash:
- 1 tbsp. of water, filtered
- 1 egg, large

Instructions:

Place the flour, 1 tsp. of salt and frozen slices of butter in food processor. Pulse off and on for 1/2 minute, till butter pieces are roughly the size of green peas.

Stir the vinegar into filtered, cold water. Drizzle this mixture into flour mixture. Pulse off and on for 10-12 seconds, till mixture holds together when pinched and has a crumbly texture.

Transfer the mixture to your work surface. Press together till you have a dough lump. Wrap with cling wrap and set in refrigerator to chill for an hour or longer.

Mix pinch of kosher salt with Canadian spice rub in small sized bowl.

Place the quartered potatoes in a medium pan. Cover with filtered, cold water, then add 1 tsp. salt. Bring to boil on high, then reduce the heat level to med-low. Simmer for 10-15 minutes, till cooked fully through. Scoop potatoes out. Transfer to bowl. Reserve the cooking liquid. Then mash the potatoes.

Melt butter in large skillet on med. heat. Add onion pieces and pinch of kosher salt. Stir while cooking for 10-15 minutes, till onions have turned golden.

Stir the spice blend, garlic and celery into skillet where onions still remain. Stir for 1/2 minute, till the onion mixture becomes coated evenly with the spices. Add veal and beef. Ladle 3/4 cup of cooking liquid from potatoes into skillet.

Stir while cooking till meat has browned and has a texture almost like paste. Continue to stir occasionally while cooking for 45-50 minutes, till most liquid is evaporated and meat becomes tender. Add mashed potatoes and stir.

Remove skillet from the heat. Allow to cool a bit.

Preheat the oven to 375F.

Working on floured work surface, divide chilled ball of dough in two pieces, one a bit larger, one a bit smaller. Roll larger dough piece into 12" circle. Place in 9" pie plate, deep-dish type. Roll out top crust into 11" circle. Cut slits in top crust so steam can escape.

Fill the bottom crust with meat mixture and smooth surface. Whisk the water and egg together. Brush bottom crust edges with this egg wash. Place the top crust on top of filling. Press lightly, sealing edges. Trim away any excess dough. Crimp crust edges. Brush the entire pie surface with the egg wash.

Place pie in 375F oven. Bake for 55-60 minutes, till browned well. Allow to cool a bit and serve.

5 – Quebec-Style Poutine

Despite any differences that residents of Quebec may have otherwise, they nearly all love poutine. It's a comforting and hearty combination of cheese curds and potato fries topped with savory gravy.

Makes 4 Servings

Cooking + Prep Time: 1/2 hour

Ingredients:

- To fry: 1 quart of oil, vegetable
- 1 x 10 & 1/4-oz. can of gravy, beef, low sodium
- 5 fry-cut potatoes, medium
- 2 cups of curds, cheese

Instructions:

Heat vegetable oil in deep skillet or deep fryer till temperature is 365F. Warm the gravy.

Place potato fries in hot oil. Cook for 5-6 minutes, till light brown. Drain on paper towels.

Place fries on serving platter. Sprinkle with cheese curds. Ladle over the top with gravy. Serve promptly.

6 – Montreal Caramelized Apples

These apples are usually made a bit sweet but not too sugary. You can pop them into pre-made tart shells for a quick and easy side dish.

Makes 6 Servings

Cooking + Prep Time: 25 minutes

Ingredients:

- 3 tbsp. of unsalted butter
- 5 peeled, 1/2"-cubed apples, Honeycrisp, Crispin, Jonagold or similar
- 1 tbsp. + 2 tbsp. of sugar, granulated
- 1/2 tsp. of cinnamon, ground
- 1/4 tsp. of lemon zest, fresh
- 1/3 cup of cider, apple, store-bought is fine

Instructions:

Melt butter in large-sized skillet on med. heat.

Add apples. Sprinkle in 1 tbsp. of sugar.

Stir apples frequently while sautéing till they start turning tender, 6-8 minutes. Don't overcook the apples.

Sprinkle apples using remainder of sugar, then lemon zest and cinnamon. Gently toss mixture. Cook on med. heat for 2 more minutes, till apples have become crisp-tender and sugar has started caramelizing. Transfer apples to serving bowl.

Raise heat to high. Add cider to skillet and scrape up browned bits, if any. Reduce heat level a bit. Allow pan juices and cider to gently simmer for 1-3 minutes, till sauce has thickened and reduced.

Pour this sauce over warmed apples. Serve promptly.

7 – Quebec Meatball & Pork Shank Stew

This stew is known in French as "Ragout de Pattes de Cochon." It's a rich and hearty dish, originally made from a French recipe.

Makes 4 Servings

Cooking + Prep Time: 3 & 1/2 hours

Ingredients:

For the Stew:

- 1 tbsp. of sea salt, coarse. +/- as desired
- 1/2 tsp. of cinnamon, ground
- 1/4 tsp. of cloves, ground
- 1/4 tsp. of pepper, ground
- 1/8 tsp. of nutmeg, ground
- 1/8 tsp. of salt, garlic
- 2 shanks, pork
- 2 tbsp. of oil, olive
- Water, sufficient to cover ingredients
- 1 chunk-cut onion, large
- 1 chopped celery stalk

For the Meatballs:

- 1 & 1/2 lb. of pork, ground
- 1 finely chopped onion, small
- 2 tbsp. of parsley, chopped
- 1/4 tsp. of cinnamon, ground
- 1/4 tsp. of cloves, ground
- 1/4 tsp. of ginger, ground
- 1/4 tsp. of powdered mustard
- 1/4 tsp. of salt, kosher
- 1/4 tsp. of pepper, ground
- 2/3 cup of flour, toasted
- 2 tbsp. of oil, olive

Instructions:

Mix the sea salt with 1/4 tsp. pepper, 1/4 tsp. of cloves, 1/2 tsp. of cinnamon, garlic salt and nutmeg in medium bowl. Rub this mixture over all parts of pork shanks.

Heat 2 tbsp. oil in large pan. Cook pork shanks in heated oil for 2-3 minutes each side till browned. Add water to cover shanks. Add celery and onions. Bring to boil. Simmer for 2-3 hours, till pork falls easily from bones.

Transfer shanks to cutting board and shred the pork.

Strain the liquid from cooking and discard bones, celery and onions. Pour this strained mixture back in pan. Stir in pork shreds.

Mix the ground pork with onions, parsley, 1/4 tsp. each cinnamon, cloves & ground pepper, plus kosher salt, mustard powder and ginger in large-sized bowl. Shape the mixture in balls.

Pour the toasted flour in shallow, wide dish and roll the meatballs in it.

Heat 2 tbsp. of oil in large-sized skillet on med-high. Cook the meatballs in small batches for 1-2 minutes each side, till browned.

Add meatballs into pork stew. Stir in the excess flour and simmer for 25-30 minutes, till stew thickens and meatballs aren't pink in middle anymore. Serve.

8 – French Canadian Gougeres

Gougeres are simple cheese puffs, and they're typically served with cocktails or wine as a tasty appetizer. They're very easy to make, which makes them quite popular.

Makes 10 Servings

Cooking + Prep Time: 45 minutes

Ingredients:

- 1 cup of water, filtered
- 8 tbsp. of 1/2"-cubed butter, unsalted
- 1/2 tsp. of salt, kosher
- 1 cup of all-purpose flour
- 4 eggs, large
- 1 & 1/2 cups of cheese, shredded Gruyere
- 3 tbsp. of cheese, grated Parmesan
- 1/8 tsp. of nutmeg, grated freshly

- 1/4 tsp. of pepper, black

Instructions:

Preheat the oven to 375F. Line two cookie sheets with baking paper.

In large-sized pan, bring the water, salt & butter to rolling, rapid boil. Be sure all butter has melted. Add the flour.

Stir mixture till it forms a sticky ball of dough and starts pulling from pan sides, 20-30 seconds.

Reduce heat level to med-low. Stir while cooking for 1 & 1/2 minutes. Remove pan from the heat. Set aside for 6-7 minutes.

Beat the eggs in, one after another. Beat in cheeses & seasonings.

Place teaspoons full of mixture on cookie sheets with an inch between them. Bake in 375F oven for 25-30 minutes, and rotate position of cookie sheets halfway done. When gougeres are puffed and golden brown, they are done. Serve.

9 – Quebec-Style Maple Baked Beans

This bean dish is easy to make, and it's the perfect harmony of savory and sweet. The sweetness of the molasses and maple is balanced by the Worcestershire sauce and tomatoes.

Makes 4 Servings

Cooking + Prep Time: 15 minutes

Ingredients:

- 1 x 19-oz. can of beans, navy or cannellini
- 1 finely chopped onion, small
- 1/2 tbsp. of oil, olive
- 1/3 cup of tomatoes, crushed
- 2 tbsp. of molasses, pure
- 2 tbsp. of syrup, maple
- 1 tbsp. of mustard, spicy, brown or Dijon
- 1 tbsp. of lemon juice, fresh
- 1 tsp. of Worcestershire sauce, reduced sodium

- 1/2 tsp. of paprika, sweet
- Salt, kosher & pepper, ground, as desired
- 1/4 to 1/2 cup of water, filtered

Instructions:

Heat the oil in large skillet over med. heat. Add onions. Let them cook over med-low till they caramelize, 8-10 minutes.

Drain can of its beans. Rinse them using tap water and add beans to skillet.

Add tomatoes, syrup, molasses, lemon juice, mustard, paprika, Worcestershire sauce, kosher salt & ground pepper (as desired). Combine over med. heat.

Reduce heat level to low. Allow mixture to simmer over low heat level for 5-6 minutes and add a little water if your sauce seems thicker than you'd like. Serve.

10 – French Canadian Bagels

The bagels common to Quebec are thinner and smaller than those in, say, New York, and they're usually shaped without cutters. They typically are just a bit sweet from the maple syrup or honey included in the dough.

Makes 8 Servings

Cooking + Prep Time: 3 & 1/2 hours

Ingredients:

For the Dough:

- 1 cup of water, lukewarm
- 2 tsp. of syrup, maple
- 2 tsp. of yeast, active dry or instant
- 3 & 1/4 – 3 & 1/2 cups of bread flour, unbleached
- 1 tsp. of salt, kosher

For the Topping:

- 3/4 cup of poppy or sesame seeds
- 3 quarts of water, filtered

- 1/3 cup of honey, pure

Instructions:

To prepare dough, combine all ingredients. Use lower flour amount and mix till you have formed a firm dough.

Use last 1/4 cup of flour if needed and hand-knead dough for 10-12 minutes. You want an elastic, smooth dough that isn't sticky. Place your dough in greased, glass bowl. Cover with cling wrap. Allow to rise for 1 & 1/2 hours, till its bulk nearly doubles.

Line cookie sheet with baking paper. Place poppy or sesame seeds in shallow, wide bowl.

After dough has risen, deflate it and divide it in eight pieces of roughly equal size.

Roll pieces into 6-inch ropes. Wrap ropes one at a time around fingers. Overlap ends. Seal by rolling your palm over seam.

Place bagels on cookie sheet and cover. Let them rise as you're setting up your boiling liquid. Preheat oven and baking stone inside to 475F.

Fill large pan with three inches of filtered water. Add honey. Place on med-high. Bring water up to boil.

After bagels have risen a bit, they're ready to be cooked.

Reduce heat level of water to simmer. Slip 2 or 3 bagels in it. Cook on the first side for one minute. Flip and cook other side for a minute, too.

Remove bagels and dredge in seeds. Flip cookie sheet over and place baking paper on back. Place boiled bagel rounds back on baking paper.

Once you have boiled all bagels, slide baking paper and bagels onto baking stone. Bake at 475F till golden brown, 18-22 minutes. Remove bagels from oven. Cool on rack and serve.

11 – Quebec Split Pea Soup

This soup is very different from the type you may be familiar with in the US. You may use yellow peas, and it's a heartier and more filling dish.

Makes 6 Servings

Cooking + Prep Time: 1 & 1/2 hours

Ingredients:

- 1 & 1/2 cups of rinsed, drained, dried split peas, green or yellow
- 1 chopped onion, medium
- 1 chopped leek, medium
- 1 chopped celery stalk
- 1 chopped carrot
- 2 minced garlic cloves
- 2 tbsp. of oil, olive
- 1 tsp. of savory, dried
- 2 fresh bay leaves, medium
- 4 cups of broth, chicken

- 2 cups of water, filtered
- Optional: a pinch of salt, kosher
- Optional: pepper, ground, as desired

Instructions:

Rinse peas thoroughly under cold running water and then drain them. There is no need to presoak the peas.

Chop onions, leek, celery and carrot. Mince garlic.

Heat oil in pot on med. heat. Add leek and onions. Sauté while occasionally stirring for 4 to 5 minutes, till they are translucent. Add garlic, carrots, celery, bay leaves and savory. Stir occasionally while cooking for 5 minutes.

Add water, broth, peas, and salt & ground pepper as desired. Bring to boil. Reduce heat level, then simmer for an hour or more, till peas have become quite soft. Ladle in bowls. Serve.

12 – French Canadian Cauliflower Soup

This soup features roasted cauliflower, making it a healthy and delicious dish. It's not low in fat since it uses heavy cream, but it certainly is delectable.

Makes 6 Servings

Cooking + Prep Time: 35 minutes

Ingredients:

- 1 lb. of cauliflower, fresh – remove the outer leaves
- 1 potato, medium
- 2 tbsp. of butter, unsalted
- 1 peeled, roughly chopped onion, medium
- 1 peeled, crushed garlic clove
- 1/2 cup of white wine, dry
- 1 quart of stock or broth, vegetable
- Salt, kosher, as desired
- Pepper, white, as desired
- 1 tbsp. of minced chives, fresh

- 1/4 cup of heated cream, heavy

Instructions:

Cut the cauliflower in 1/2 – 1" thick pieces. Reserve 1 cup smaller florets.

Peel potato. Cut into small pieces.

In heavy soup pot, heat butter on med-low. Add cauliflower, onions and garlic. Stir continuously while cooking for 2-3 minutes, till onion becomes a bit translucent.

Add wine. Cook for 1-2 minutes more, till wine is reduced by 1/2 or so.

Add stock and potato pieces. Raise heat level to med-high. Bring to boil. Reduce heat, then simmer for 15-18 minutes, till potatoes and cauliflower have softened somewhat. Don't allow them to become mushy.

Heat sauté pan with a bit of olive oil. Sauté reserved florets of cauliflower till tender. Season as desired.

Remove pan from the heat. Puree in food processor. Return soup to pot. Bring back up to simmer. Add additional stock or broth if you need to thin the soup at all. Add the heated cream. Season as desired.

Portion soup in small, individual bowls, and garnish them with chives and reserved florets. Serve promptly.

13 – Slow Cooker-Style Ham with Maple Syrup & Beer

Ham is one of the favorite meats in Canada, especially for the meals during the holiday season. This Quebec-style version is made with beer and maple syrup.

Makes 8 Servings

Cooking + Prep Time: 15 minutes + 10 to 12 hours slow cooker time

Ingredients:

- 3 lb. of whole ham, smoked
- 1 tbsp. of mustard powder
- 1/2 cup of syrup, maple
- 1 & 1/3 cups of lager beer
- Optional: pepper, ground, as desired

Instructions:

Place ham in large-sized pot. Cover using cold, filtered water. Bring to boil and allow to simmer for 10 minutes. Drain thoroughly.

Transfer ham to slow cooker. Add remainder of ingredients. Cover slow cooker with lid. Cook on the low setting for 10 to 12 hours, till meat is fall-apart tender. Season as desired and serve.

14 – Montreal-Style Cranberry Relish

This tangy and colorful relish is a wonderful addition to your holiday dinner table. It's a nice change from the typical cranberry sauce, too.

Makes Various # of Servings

Cooking + Prep Time: 15 minutes

Ingredients:

- 12 oz. of frozen or fresh cranberries
- 1/3 cup of sugar, granulated
- 1 zested, juiced fresh orange, medium
- 1 apple, small
- Allspice, as desired

Instructions:

Grate orange zest. Add orange juice and zest to food processor. Add cranberries, sugar and allspice, too.

Process berry mixture for 10-15 minutes till berries have been chopped well and combined thoroughly with orange juice, zest and sugar. You want small pieces, not a mushy mixture.

Peel, then core apple. Cut in slivers or cubes. Combine with other ingredients in large-sized bowl. Serve. Can be stored up to 1 day in refrigerator or frozen for 3-4 months.

15 – Savory Chicken Pies

Individual meat pies are a popular food in Quebec. They're available at most supermarkets there. This recipe is healthier than the pot pies you can buy premade and tastier, too.

Makes 8 Servings

Cooking + Prep Time: 1 hour & 5 minutes

Ingredients:

- 4 peeled, diced carrots, medium
- 1 cup of peas, frozen
- 2 finely chopped onions, medium
- 2 minced garlic cloves
- 2/3 cup of unsalted butter
- 1 cup of flour, all-purpose
- 4 cups of chicken broth, canned, low sodium
- 4 cups of chicken, boiled, prepared
- 2 diced celery stalks

- Optional: a pinch of salt, kosher
- Optional: pepper, ground, as desired
- 1 box of pastry dough, puff type

Instructions:

Preheat oven to 375F.

Blanch the diced carrots and frozen peas for 5 minutes or so in a small pot with lightly salted, boiling water. Drain carrots and peas and set them aside.

Melt butter in pan on med. heat. Add garlic and onions. Sauté till translucent, 3 to 4 minutes. Add flour. Cook while stirring for 2 minutes. Add broth while stirring. Bring to boil. Add chicken pieces, diced celery, carrots and peas. Season as desired. Cook for several minutes. Transfer mixture into small baking dishes. Set aside.

On lightly floured board, roll pastry out in 14" x 14" +/- squares with rolling pin. Cut out four discs with same diameter as small baking dishes. Place atop dishes.

Bake in center rack of 375F oven for 1/2 hour. Serve.

16 – French Canadian Onion Soup

This onion soup has been a favorite comfort food in Quebec for many years. The caramelized soft onions will be cooked in a rich stock, making a delicious dish.

Makes 4 Servings

Cooking + Prep Time: 45 minutes

Ingredients:

- 2 cups of sliced onions
- 1 tbsp. of butter, unsalted
- 3/4 cup of white wine, dry
- 1 quart of broth, chicken or vegetable, low sodium
- A pinch of nutmeg, grated, +/- as desired
- A dash of pepper, ground, +/- as desired
- Salt, kosher, as needed/desired
- 4 bread slices, French
- 1/2 cup of cheese, gruyere – you can substitute gouda if you like

Instructions:

Sauté the onion slices in 1 tbsp. of butter on med. heat, stirring occasionally, till they begin turning a golden brown, 13-15 minutes.

Add 3/4 cup of wine and 1 quart of broth. Bring to boil, then reduce the heat level. Simmer gently for 15 to 20 minutes.

Grate nutmeg into soup as desired. Add a bit of ground pepper. Taste and adjust seasoning, as desired.

As soup cooks, toast 8 bread slices in toaster oven.

Scoop soup into oven-safe individual bowls. Add 1 slice toasted bread each. Sprinkle 2 tbsp. cheese atop them and place bowls on baking sheet. Broil till cheese has melted and turned a little brown. Serve.

17 – Shepherd's Pie

Most every cook in Quebec likely has shepherd's pie recipes in their cookbook. Everyone makes them just a bit differently, but the taste is always amazing.

Makes 6 Servings

Cooking + Prep Time: 1 hour

Ingredients:

- 5 peeled, halved potatoes, medium
- 1 & 1/2 finely chopped onions, medium
- 16 thinly sliced mushrooms, button
- 2 tbsp. of oil, olive
- 1 lb. of beef, ground, lean
- 3/4 cup of diced tomatoes, canned
- 2 tbsp. of tomato paste, no salt added
- 1 tbsp. of Worcestershire sauce, reduced sodium
- 1 cup of broth, beef, low sodium

- 1 cup of peas, frozen
- 1 cup of 2% milk
- 2 tbsp. of unsalted butter
- Optional: pepper, ground, as desired
- Optional: a pinch of salt, kosher

Instructions:

Preheat oven to 400F.

Chop onions and slice mushrooms thinly. Peel and halve the potatoes. Boil them in filtered water till quite tender, 20 to 25 minutes. Drain well. Set potatoes aside.

Heat oil in pan on med-high. Add ground meat. Sear for 4 to 5 minutes, till meat loses red color. Break up using a fork.

When meat has turned a golden color, add onions. Stir while cooking for 2 minutes. Add and stir in mushrooms, tomatoes, Worcestershire sauce, broth and tomato paste.

Add frozen peas. Continue to cook for 4 to 5 minutes till heated fully through. Season as desired. Remove pan from heat. Transfer mixture to a large-sized casserole dish.

Pour milk into micro-wave safe bowl and add butter. Microwave on the med-high setting uncovered for several minutes, till quite hot. Add cooked potatoes. Mash mixture till it's creamy. Season as desired. Place a spoon full of potato mixture atop beef mixture. Spread gently and evenly cover beef mixture.

Bake in middle rack of 400F oven for 30-35 minutes, till top turns golden-brown. Serve.

18 – Montreal Pork Pie

This Quebec pork pie is flavorful and simple, and it makes a cozy dinner. You can serve it while hot or warm or allow it to cool before serving.

Makes 8 Servings

Cooking + Prep Time: 1 hour & 35 minutes

Ingredients:

- 2 pie crusts, prepared
- 2 lb. of pork, ground
- 1 diced onion, medium
- 1 tsp. of salt, kosher
- 1/3 cup of water, filtered
- 3/4 tsp. of allspice, ground
- 3/4 tsp. of cloves, ground
- 3 cups of potatoes, mashed
- 1 tbsp. of milk, 2%

Instructions:

In medium skillet on med. heat, combine pork, onions, water and salt. Stir often while simmering for 15-20 minutes, till all the liquid has evaporated. Add potatoes. Combine by beating.

Preheat oven to 400F.

Dust your work surface with flour. Then roll out two pie crusts. Line pie plate with one and add pork and potato mixture. Add second crust to top. Flute edges. Brush top crust using milk. Use a fork to prick top crust.

Bake in 400F oven for 25-35 minutes, till crust turns golden brown. Serve.

19 – Quebec Pork Roast

This recipe was handed down through generations of a French family to French Canadian families. Be sure not to leave out the ketchup, which is what makes the dish uniquely delicious.

Makes 6 Servings

Cooking + Prep Time: 2 hours & 20 minutes

Ingredients:

- 3 pounds of beef, roast
- 1 tbsp. of flour, all-purpose
- 1 tsp. of salt, sea
- 1 tsp. of pepper, ground
- 2 tbsp. of oil, vegetable
- 2 minced garlic cloves
- 1/4 tsp. of thyme, dried
- 1/4 tsp. of rosemary, dried
- 1/4 tsp. of marjoram, dried

- 1/4 tsp. of mustard, dry
- 1/4 cup of ketchup, no salt added
- 1 cup of dry wine, red
- 1/4 cup of water, filtered
- 1 bay leaf, fresh
- 1/2 pound of fresh mushrooms, small

Instructions:

Rub all over the roast with flour, kosher salt & ground pepper.

Heat the oil in a non-stick, deep pan.

Add beef to heated oil. Turn often while browning on med. heat for 10-12 minutes. Reduce heat level to low. Add water, wine, bay leaf, ketchup, mustard and herbs. Season with sea salt & ground pepper, as desired.

Cover pan. Cook for an hour and a half.

Add liquid if the roast boils dry. Add mushrooms and cover pan again. Simmer till meat becomes tender, 30-35 minutes. Serve with gravy and mushrooms.

20 – Montreal Squash Bisque

The butternut squash used in this recipe has a mild sweetness and is offset well by the fresh savory herbs. The heavy cream makes the texture velvety and creates a thick and rich bisque.

Makes 6 Servings

Cooking + Prep Time: 45 minutes

Ingredients:

- 1 chopped, medium onion, yellow
- 1/2 cup of celery, chopped finely
- 1/2 tsp. of chopped thyme, fresh
- 1/2 tsp. of crushed rosemary, fresh
- 1 chopped sage leaf, fresh
- 2 tbsp. of oil, olive
- 1 tsp. of salt, kosher
- 1/4 tsp. of pepper, ground
- 1 peeled, cubed butternut squash, medium

- 2 & 1/4 cups of stock, chicken
- 1 cup of heavy cream
- For garnishing: croutons, unseasoned

Instructions:

In large pan on med. heat, sauté onions, thyme, celery, sage and rosemary in oil till vegetables become tender, 5-7 minutes.

Add kosher salt & ground pepper. Sauté vegetables with herbs for two minutes more.

Add stock and squash to pan. Bring soup up to a simmer.

Reduce heat a bit. Cover pan. Simmer till squash becomes tender, 15-20 minutes.

Puree soup with immersion blender till thoroughly smooth. Stir in cream and heat fully through. Garnish with croutons and serve while hot.

21 – Quebec Maple Smash Drink

This traditional drink has a twist of maple, and it's easy to prepare. The robust syrup perfectly complements the fruit juices.

Makes 1 Serving

Cooking + Prep Time: 5-7 minutes

Ingredients:

- 1/4 cup of whiskey, Canadian
- 1/8 cup of lemon juice, fresh
- A dash of bitters, grapefruit
- 2 & 1/2 tsp. of syrup, maple, the darker the better
- 8 to 10 leaves of mint, fresh

Instructions:

Add the whiskey, bitters, lemon juice & syrup to shaker cup with crushed ice.

Shake till shaker becomes frosty, about 10 seconds.

Strain into rocks glass. Use crushed ice to top.

Use mint sprig for garnish and serve.

22 – Canadian Brie & Syrup

This is a favorite at parties in Quebec. There are only a few ingredients, too, so it's a breeze to prepare.

Makes Various # of Servings

Cooking + Prep Time: 20 minutes

Ingredients:

- 14 ounces of cheese, Brie
- 1 cup of chopped walnut pieces
- 2 cups of syrup, maple, pure
- 1 x 3/4"-sliced baguette bread loaf, French

Instructions:

Preheat the oven to 200F.

Place unwrapped Brie in baking dish and sprinkle the top with chopped walnut pieces. Pour syrup over cheese and nuts both.

Bake in 200F oven till cheese has warmed and softened, 8-10 minutes. Serve the cheese with baguette slices.

23 – Quebec Garlic Soup

Our friends have been delighted with this garlic soup's texture and taste. It's a bit different than the original, which goes back many years, but the changes are minor.

Makes 6 Servings

Cooking + Prep Time: 45 minutes

Ingredients:

- 4 minced garlic cloves
- 4 tbsp. of oil, olive
- 3 cups of cubed bread, fresh – remove the crust
- 1 tsp. of paprika, sweet
- 3 cups of water, filtered
- 2 cups of stock, chicken
- 1/4 tsp. of pepper, cayenne, +/- as desired
- 1/2 tsp. of salt, kosher
- 2 eggs, large

- 1 tbsp. of parsley, chopped

Instructions:

Heat oil with garlic in large pot over low heat till it has become transparent. Be careful that you don't burn garlic.

Add cubed bread. Mix till incorporated well, so they absorb oil completely.

Add remainder of ingredients with the exception or parsley and eggs. Bring to boil.

Reduce the heat level. Simmer for 25-30 minutes.

Thoroughly blend soup with whisk till very smooth.

Beat eggs lightly. Gradually add them to soup. Simmer for two more minutes, then serve.

24 – French Canadian Cheese Fondue

There is something simple and rewarding about spearing crusty break chunks from a bubbly pot of heated cheese. Fondues are not difficult to prepare, and they involve everyone in the serving.

Makes Various # of Servings

Cooking + Prep Time: 35 minutes

Ingredients:

- 4 oz. of cheese, grated coarsely – Emmental or Swiss
- 4 oz. of cheese, gruyere, grated coarsely
- 1 tbsp. of flour, all-purpose
- A pinch of nutmeg, ground
- 1 pinch of pepper, black
- 3/4 cup of white wine, dry
- 1 halved garlic clove
- 1 tbsp. of brandy, cherry
- Dippers like vegetables, bread cubes, etc.

Instructions:

Place the cheese in large-sized bowl. Sprinkle it with nutmeg, pepper and flour. Toss well so flour coats cheese evenly.

Cut bread in bite-sized chunks.

Heat the wine in medium pot on med-high till small bubbles start rising to surface.

Add cheese to the wine slowly. Allow one handful to fully melt before you add another.

After cheese has melted fully, add the brandy. Rub fondue pot inside with sliced side of the garlic clove.

Transfer mixture into fondue pot. Keep the flame hot enough so it keeps the cheese melted but does not boil it. Serve with dippers.

25 – French Onion Pie

The traditional name of this dish is Tarte a l'oignon. It's typically served during the holiday season, but it goes great for potluck dinners, too.

Makes 10 Servings

Cooking + Prep Time: 1 hour & 25 minutes

Ingredients:

- 10 bacon slices – cut in 1" pieces
- 5 thinly sliced onions, medium
- 1 tsp. of salt, kosher
- 1/8 tsp. of pepper, ground
- 1/2 cup of milk, whole
- 1/2 cup of cream, heavy
- 1 tbsp. of flour, all-purpose
- 4 eggs, large
- A pinch of nutmeg, ground
- 1 x 9" pie crust, prepared

Instructions:

Preheat the oven to 400F.

Place bacon in skillet. Cook on med. heat till it browns. Remove the bacon from skillet and reserve 4 tbsp. of bacon fat. Drain bacon on the paper towels.

Place onions in skillet with bacon fat. Cook on med-high for 6-8 minute, till browned evenly. Season as desired.

Combine cream and milk in medium bowl. Sprinkle flour over onions. Stir, blending well. Add milk mixture and stir again.

Stir while mixture is cooking on med. heat, till it has thickened. Remove skillet from the heat. Add and stir bacon. Set aside and allow to cool for 8-10 minutes.

Beat eggs in medium bowl till frothy and lightly colored. Stir in one spoon full of onion mixture. Add second spoon of onion mixture. Continue to stir. Repeat till all onions are stirred into eggs and have blended well. Pour mixture into pie shell and sprinkle the top with ground nutmeg.

Bake in 400F oven for 18-20 minutes, till crust has browned lightly. Remove from oven. Allow to cool for 5-7 minutes and serve.

Check out these Delectable Desserts from Quebec…

26 – French Canadian Cinnamon Pastry

These delicious pastries, also known as Pêtes de Soeur, are typically made with pie dough, butter, cinnamon, and brown sugar. The name comes from the fact that it was once served at Quebec boarding schools by the nuns who taught there.

Makes 36 Pastries

Cooking + Prep Time: 1 hour & 10 minutes + 1 hour chilling time

Ingredients:

- 3 cups of flour, all-purpose
- 1 cup of lard, as needed
- 1/2 tsp. of salt, kosher
- 1 beaten egg, large
- 5 tbsp. of water, cold, filtered
- 1 tsp. of vinegar, balsamic
- Butter – as needed for spreading on dough
- 1 & 1/2 cups of sugar, brown

- 2 tsp. of cinnamon, ground

Instructions:

Preheat oven to 350F.

Cut flour, sufficient lard and kosher salt together till the consistency is like that of small peas.

Combine water, vinegar and egg. Add gradually to the flour mixture from step 2.

Stir till the mixture is barely moistened and forms a soft-textured dough.

Wrap the dough and place in refrigerator for one hour.

Roll the dough out in two squares. Spread butter over entire area. Evenly sprinkle dough with cinnamon and brown sugar.

Roll dough into shapes like logs. Them cut them in pinwheels of 1/2" thickness. Place on cookie sheets lined with baking paper.

Bake in 350F oven for 18-20 minutes. Allow to completely cool, then serve.

27 – Apple Cider Quebec Pound Cake

This tender cake is often served with a cup of tea or latte. You can also serve it with a bit of vanilla ice cream if you like.

Makes 16 Servings

Cooking + Prep Time: 1 hour & 55 minutes

Ingredients:

- 3 cups of cider, apple
- 2 tbsp. of syrup, maple
- 2 cups of sugar, granulated
- 1 & 1/2 cups of room temperature butter, unsalted
- 2 tsp. of vanilla extract
- 6 room temperature eggs, large
- 3 cups of flour, all-purpose
- 1 tsp. of cinnamon, ground
- 1/2 tsp. of baking powder, pure
- 1/2 tsp. of nutmeg, grated

- 1/2 tsp. of allspice, ground
- 1/4 tsp. of salt, kosher
- 1/4 tsp. of cloves, ground

Instructions:

Bring cider to boil in medium pan on med-high. Continue to boil for 25-35 minutes, till volume is reduced to a bit less than a cup. Remove cider from heat. Add maple syrup and set mixture aside.

Preheat oven to 325F. Lightly grease 10" Bundt-style cake pan. Set aside.

Cream butter, vanilla and sugar till mixture is fluffy and light. Add eggs, one after another, and beat for several seconds after you add each egg.

Stir remainder of dry ingredients together. Add 1/2 of this mixture to creamed mixture created in step 3. Beat till you have incorporated most of the flour.

Add cooled syrup/cider reduction to batter. Beat for 1/2 minute. Beat in last 1/2 of dry ingredient mixture.

Spread batter into pan prepared above. Bake in 325F oven for an hour & 10-12 minutes, till you can insert a toothpick near middle and have it come back clean.

Cool cake in pan on wire rack for 8 to 10 minutes. Shake it a bit, loosening sides and bottom from pan. Place platter over top of cake. Invert it and remove pan. Allow it to finish cooling and serve.

28 – French Canadian Maple Syrup Pie

This is a delicious pie, very emblematic of the desserts in Quebec, the home of maple syrup. The cream balances the dessert's sweetness and complements its silkiness.

Makes 8-10 Servings

Cooking + Prep Time: 2 hours & 35 minutes

Ingredients:

- 1 pie crust, prepared
- 1 & 1/2 cups of packed sugar, light brown
- 2 room temperature eggs, large
- 1/2 cup of cream, heavy
- 1/3 cup of maple syrup, pure
- 2 tsp. of melted butter, unsalted
- For serving: whipped cream, unsweetened or crème fraîche

Instructions:

Preheat the oven to 350F.

Fit the pie crust into 8" pie plate & trim away excess dough. Decoratively crimp the edges.

Whisk eggs and brown sugar together till creamy. Next, add the cream, butter and syrup. Whisk till you have a smooth consistency. Pour pie filling into shell in pie plate.

Bake pie on lower rack of 350F oven for 50-60 minutes till pastry turns golden. Filling should puff up and appear dry, but it should still jiggle. Cool on rack and allow filling to set. Serve.

29 – Quebec Sugar Pie

Also known as "Tarte au sucre," this sugar pie will be a welcome change at Thanksgiving dinner, but you can serve it any time. Topping it with some whipped cream & strawberries or toasted nuts makes it as pretty as it is tasty.

Makes 12 Servings

Cooking + Prep Time: 50 minutes

Ingredients:

- 1 pie crust, prepared

For the Filling:

- 1/4 cup of flour, all-purpose, unbleached
- 1 & 1/2 cups of packed sugar, light brown
- 1 egg, large
- 1 yolk from separate large egg
- 1 & 1/2 cups of whipping cream, heavy

For the Topping:

- 1 & 1/2 cups of cream, heavy
- 1 tsp. of vanilla extract, pure
- Strawberries, fresh

Instructions:

Preheat oven temperature to 350F.

Whisk flour & sugar together well. Beat egg and egg yolk in small sized bowl. Add eggs to the flour/sugar mixture. Whisk together well.

Add the cream to a small pan. Bring to boil. Remove from the heat.

Add the filling mixture and whisk them together.

Pour mixture through a sieve or strainer. Place tart pan with pie crust lining it onto a cookie sheet. Pour pie filling into crust.

Bake the pie in 350F oven for 33-35 minutes. Remove tart pan carefully from cookie sheet. Place it on cooling rack.

Hull strawberries and cut them in quarters. Add the cream & vanilla to medium bowl. Mix together using hand mixer. Increase speed gradually to high. Mix for 2-3 minutes, till mixture forms stiff peaks.

Top the sugar pie slices with sweet whipped cream & some strawberries. Serve.

30 – French Canadian Poor Man's Pudding

"Pouding Chomeur" translates to "unemployment pudding." Actually, though, it is not inexpensive to make. It's a wonderful dessert, especially when paired with ice cream or summer fruits.

Makes 10 Servings

Cooking + Prep Time: 55 minutes

Ingredients:

For the Syrup:

- 2 cups of cream, heavy
- 2 cups of syrup, maple

For the Batter:

- 3/4 cup of room temperature butter, unsalted
- 3/4 cup of sugar, granulated
- 1/4 tsp. of vanilla extract, pure
- 2 room temperature eggs, large
- 1 tsp. of baking powder, pure
- 1 & 3/4 cups of flour, all-purpose

- 1/2 tsp. of salt, fine

Instructions:

Preheat oven to 425F. Butter deep glass baking dish. Place on cookie sheet.

Bring cream and syrup to boil in deep pan on med-high. Once mixture begins bubbling, turn heat off and set pan aside.

Beat the butter & granulated sugar together in medium bowl with electric mixer till well-combined and creamy. Add and whisk 1 egg and vanilla till incorporated well. Mix in second egg. Add baking powder, flour and salt. Use a spatula to mix till barely combined.

Transfer the batter to dish prepared above. Pour creamy maple sauce over the top. Don't fill dish to the top. Leave 1/2" – 1" empty above sauce. Reserve extra sauce, if any.

Bake on center rack of 425F oven for 1/2 hour, till the pudding has turned golden brown. If you insert a toothpick in middle, it should come back almost clean. Allow to cool for 8-10 minutes. Serve with reserved creamy maple sauce.

Conclusion

This Quebec cookbook has shown you…

How to use different ingredients to affect unique French Canadian tastes in many dishes.

How can you include Canadian recipes in your home repertoire?

You can…

Make breakfasts of cretons with toast and maple syrup grandfathers, which you may not have heard of them before. They are just as mouthwatering tasty as they sound.

Cook the stews and soups, often served in French Canadian homes. You can find their suitable ingredients in frozen food, meat or produce sections in local supermarkets.

Enjoy making the tastiest Quebec meat dishes, including beef, veal and pork. Meat is a favorite in the recipes, with a good reason.

Make the dishes using fresh vegetables in Canadian recipes. There is something about the ingredients that makes the dishes more comforting.

Make the desserts like sugar pie and apple cider pound cake, which are tasty and tempting for your dinner guests.

Share the special recipes with your friends!

Thank You!

thank you

This won't be my last book, in fact, there are many books coming soon. So, thank you for getting this book because you will see with your own eyes, smell, and taste that my recipes are worth buying. Your cooking skills will get better and you will have different dishes to serve daily.

I appreciate you for choosing my work, I know you won't be disappointed. Now it's time to try out the recipes and share your experience. Leave feedback so that not only others will know about it but also, I'll be able to become even better in my work, every feedback is welcomed.

Thank you once more for choosing my book

Have an amazing day

Printed in Poland
by Amazon Fulfillment
Poland Sp. z o.o., Wrocław